BUSHRANGER BALLADS

THE WILD COLONIAL BOY
oil on hardboard 45 cm x 35 cm 1976

BUSHRANGER BALLADS

Selected and with an introduction by Bill Scott
Illustrated by Pro Hart

URE SMITH
SYDNEY AUCKLAND

First published 1976 by
Ure Smith, Sydney
a division of Books for Pleasure Pty Ltd
176 South Creek Road, Dee Why West, Australia 2099

Designed by Robin Voigt
Typesetting by G.T. Setters Pty Ltd, Sydney
Printed in Singapore by Kyodo Shing-Loong Printing Industries Pte Ltd
112 Neythal Road, Jurong town, Singapore 22

National Library of Australia Card Number and
ISBN 0 7254 0296 2

Contents

THE BALLAD OF JACK LEFROY (detail)
oil on hardboard 35 cm x 45 cm 1976

Introduction

Highwaymen in Australia could be said to fall roughly into two classes, and these might be described, for convenience, as either "bolters" or "wild colonial boys". Historically speaking, the "bolters" came first, and they seem to have set some of the traditions under which the later outlaws operated. A study of the history of the penal colonies of New South Wales and Tasmania soon shows why these two States abounded in the "bolter" type of outlaw. The term "bushranger" seems first to have been used to describe those convicts who left their assigned employment and fled to the bush, preferring possible starvation in the hostile land or murder at the hands of Aborigines to a continuing life of flogging, overwork and scanty rations. Magistrates in Sydney and surrounding districts were often so severe in their punishment of petty offences that at one time the newspaper, the *Monitor*, accused the Reverend Samuel Marsden and his fellow magistrates of "manufacturing bushrangers". There was a saying among Sydney convicts, "May the Lord have mercy on your soul, for His Reverence will have none!"

It is not surprising that these "bolters" were much admired by their fellow convicts, who helped them stay free by providing information about their pursuers, and gifts of food when they could spare it. The early bushrangers like Jack Donohoe, Mike Howe, Martin Cash, Paddy Curran, Jackey-Jackey, Matthew Brady and the Jew-boy Gang could not have remained free for so long if it had not been for their supporters and sympathizers. With few exceptions these men were heartless villains, their careers were short and their deaths usually violent. But they established the tradition of 'dying game', preferring death to capture, and also the tradition of support from sympathizers that enabled the later "wild boys" to remain at large for long periods.

The golden age of Australian bushranging, if one may call it that, began with the discovery of gold in Australia about the middle of the nineteenth century. The men who became outlaws in this period were not transportees like the "bolters". They were mostly native-born and bush-bred, magnificent horsemen from childhood. To them, the bush was not a desperate alternative to slavery. It was their home, and they loved it.

Most of them seem to have begun their careers of outlawry as horse or cattle thieves. Much as young people steal motor cars today to go "joy-riding", so these boys seem to have stolen blood horses from squatters' stables for the thrill of riding a good beast; or to have stolen cattle and sold them to pay for a spree in a wayside pub. Many poor families in the bush were descended from convict stock, and popular opinion among them regarded squatters as fair game. They seemed to equate squatters with the officials who had ruled the convict settlements so harshly. Hence their natural sympathy with those who preyed upon squatters, and their support of the outlaws with supplies and information about police movements. No doubt they were paid for their services, too.

It is also not surprising that in a population that was largely illiterate, poems and ballads grew up around the exploits of the outlaws. Most of these were composed by sympathizers. Verse and simple tune are great aids to memory of events, as witness the body of folksong in all nations. These native ballads often had little virtue as poetry, but they had a drive and simple directness of language that is their particular charm.

If one makes allowance for the probable bias of the composer, these ballads may at times give a truer account of actual happenings than contemporary newspaper reports. They may have been written by men who had the story first-hand from the participants!

When one considers the comparative size of populations, there was more outlawry in Australia than ever there was in the United States. For some twenty-five years, a well-dressed man on a fine horse stood far more chance of being "bailed up" in Australia than ever he did in Texas, Montana or Nevada. The biggest cattle theft of the century took place in the State of Queensland, and the robbers successfully drove the herd over one of the most difficult stock routes in the country to sell it in South Australia. There was so much popular admiration for the man who master-minded the operation, that he was found "Not Guilty" by a jury, despite evidence that should have sent him to gaol for many years. The Judge is reported to have said, "I thank God, gentlemen, that the verdict is yours, not mine!" before stamping from the courtroom.

Here, then, are some of the poems and ballads that were written about the bolters and wild colonial boys. There are a few by contemporary poets, but in the main they were written at the time the events described took place, and have all the sense of immediacy about them that their composition implies. For better or worse, they are part of Australia's heritage, and repay study.

Bold Jack Donohoe

'Tis of a valiant highwayman and outlaw of disdain
Who scorned to live in slavery or wear a convict's chain;
His name it was Jack Donohoe, of courage and renown—
He scorned to live in slavery or humble to the Crown.

This bold undaunted highwayman, as you may understand,
Was banished for his natural life from Erin's happy land.
In Dublin city of renown, where first his breath he drew,
It's there they titled him the brave and bold Jack Donohoe.

He scarce had been a twelvemonth on the Australian shore
When he took to the highway, as oft he had before.
Brave Macnamara, Underwood, Webber and Walmsley too,
These were the true associates of bold Jack Donohoe.

As Jack and his companions roved out one afternoon,
Not thinking that the pains of death would overcome so soon,
To their surprise five horse police appeared all in their view,
And in quick time they did advance to take Jack Donohoe.

"Come, come, you cowardly rascals, oh, do not run away!
We'll fight them man to man, my boys, their number's only three;
For I'd rather range the bush around like dingo or kangaroo
Than work one hour for Government," said bold Jack Donohoe.

"Oh, no!" said cowardly Walmsley, "to that I won't agree;
I see they're still advancing us, their number's more than three.
And if we wait, we'll be too late, the battle we will rue."
"Then begone from me, you cowardly dog," replied Jack Donohoe.

The Sergeant of the horse police discharged his carabine,
And called aloud to Donohoe, "Will you fight or resign?"
"Resign? No, no, I never will, unto your cowardly crew,
For today I'll fight with all my might!" cried bold Jack Donohoe.

The Sergeant then, in a hurry, his party to divide,
Placed one to fire in front of him, and another on each side;
The Sergeant and the Corporal, they both fired too,
Till the fatal ball had pierced the heart of bold Jack Donohoe.

Six rounds he fought with those horse police before the fatal ball,
Which pierced his heart with cruel smart, caused Donohoe to fall;
And as he closed his mournful eyes he bade this world adieu,
Saying, "Good people all, pray for the soul of poor Jack Donohoe."

There were Freincy, Grant, bold Robin Hood, Brennan and O'Hare;
With Donohoe the highwayman, none of them could compare.
But now he's gone to Heaven, I hope, with saints and angels too—
May the Lord have mercy on the soul of brave Jack Donohoe.

ANON.

Note: There are many variants of the above song, some of which are better verse than this, but as far as I know this is the earliest recorded version, and thus probably tells the story better and more faithfully than later variants. The form follows closely the broadsheets and ballads sold in the streets of England and Ireland; the first line is almost the set beginning for a highwayman ballad:

"Tis of a valiant highwayman, my story I will tell,
His name was Willy Brennan and in Ireland he did dwell", and so on.

There has been much speculation that this poem was the original of the "Wild Colonial Boy" poems. John Meredith and others have written a book and various articles about it. Private Muckleston, of the police, who fired the shot that killed Donohoe, told the inquest into his death: "... When called upon to surrender, he took off his hat, waved it three times, threw it in the air and shouted, "Come on, you bloody bastards, we're ready if there's a dozen of you...!"

BOLD JACK DONOHOE
oil on hardboard 35 cm x 45 cm 1976

A Bushranger

Jackey-Jackey gallops on a horse like a swallow
  Where the carbines bark and the blackboys hollo.
When the traps give chase (may the Devil take his power!)
  He can ride ten miles in a quarter of an hour.

Take a horse and follow, and you'll hurt no feelings;
  He can fly down waterfalls and jump through ceilings,
He can shoot off hats, for to have a bit of fun,
  With a bulldog bigger than a buffalo gun.

Honeyed and profound is his conversation
  When he bails up Mails on Long Tom Station,
In a flyaway coat with a black cravat,
  A snow white collar and a cabbage-tree hat.

Flowers in his buttonhole and pearls in his pocket,
  He comes like a ghost and he goes like a rocket
With a lightfoot heel on a blood-mare's flank
  And a bagful of notes from the Joint Stock Bank.

Many pretty ladies he could witch out of marriage,
  Though he prig but a kiss in a big-wig's carriage;
For the cock of an eye or the lift of his reins
  They would run barefoot through Patrick's Plains.

KENNETH SLESSOR

Note: Jackey-Jackey was the name given to William Westwood, who commenced his career as a ranger in 1839, in company with another villain called Paddy Curran. He soon fell out with Curran, who raped a settler's wife. Westwood disarmed him, took his horse from him, and gave him the father of a hiding for doing so, and the two men parted company. Slessor's picture of him is a faithful one; he did steal a blood mare from the Macarthurs, and wore fine clothing. He is supposed to have had a conversation with Governor Gipps at one time, but this has not been authenticated. He died miserably by hanging on Norfolk Island, after being driven almost to insanity by the treatment he received there.

A BUSHRANGER
oil on hardboard 35 cm x 45 cm 1976

The Wild Colonial Boy

'Tis of a wild colonial boy, Jack Doolan was his name,
Of poor but honest parents, he was born in Castlemaine.
He was his mother's only hope, his father's pride and joy,
And dearly did his parents love their wild colonial boy.

In sixty-one this daring youth commenced his wild career,
With a courage all undaunted, no foeman did he fear,
He stuck up the Beechworth mail coach, and robbed Judge MacEvoy,
Who trembling cold, gave up his gold to the wild colonial boy.

He bade the Judge good morning, and he told him to beware,
That he'd never rob an honest chap that acted on the square.
And never to rob a mother of her son and only joy,
In case he might turn outlaw like the wild colonial boy.

One day as he was riding the mountainside along,
A-listening to the little birds, their pleasant laughing song.
Three mounted troopers came along, Kelly, Davis and Fitzroy
With a warrant for the capture of the wild colonial boy.

"Surrender now, Jack Doolan, you see we're three to one.
Surrender in the Queen's name, you daring highwayman!"
He pulled a pistol from his belt and waved the little toy,
"I'll fight but not surrender!" said the wild colonial boy.

He fired at Trooper Kelly, and brought him to the ground,
And in return from Davis, received his mortal wound.
All shattered through the jaw he lay, still firing at Fitzroy,
And that's the way they captured him, the wild colonial boy.

So come along, my hearties, we'll roam the mountains wide,
Together we will plunder, together we will ride.
We'll gallop over mountains and scour along the plains
And scorn to live in slavery, bound down with iron chains.

ANON.

Notes would only confuse the reader. The arguments are still going on, as with "Waltzing Matilda", and no one can be sure about it now. The above version is the one I learned as a lad, or near enough to it.

THE WILD COLONIAL BOY
oil on hardboard 45 cm x 35 cm 1976

The Death of Morgan

Throughout Australia's history no tongue or pen can tell
Of such preconcerted treachery—there is no parallel—
As the tragic deed of Morgan's death; without warning he was shot
On Peechelba station, it will never be forgot.

I have oft-times heard of murders in Australia's golden land,
But such an open daylight scene of thirty in a band,
Assembled at the dawn of day, and then to separate,
Behind the trees, some on their knees, awaiting Morgan's fate.

Too busy was the servant maid, she trotted half the night
From Macpherson's down to Rutherford's the tidings to recite.
A messenger was sent away who for his neck had no regard,
He returned with a troop of traps in hopes of their reward.

But they were all disappointed; McQuinlan was the man
Who fired from his rifle and shot rebellious Dan.
Concealed he stood behind a tree till his victim came in view,
And as Morgan passed his doom was cast—the unhappy man he slew.

There was a rush for trophies, soon as the man was dead;
They cut off his beard, his ears, and the hair from off his head.
In truth it was a hideous sight as he struggled on the ground,
They tore the clothes from off his back and exposed the fatal wound.

Oh, Morgan was the traveller's friend; the squatters all rejoice
That the outlaw's life is at an end, no more they'll hear his voice.
Success attend all highwaymen who do the poor some good;
But my curse attend the treacherous man who'd shed another's blood.

Farewell to Burke, O'Meally, young Gilbert and Ben Hall,
Likewise to Daniel Morgan, who fell by rifle-ball;
So all young men be warned and never take up arms,
Remember this, how true it is, bushranging hath no charms.

ANON.

Note: "Mad Dan" Morgan was ambushed and shot by a party of 30 men on Peechelba station in Victoria, on Sunday 9 April 1865. He had held up the station the previous night, and a servant, Alice Macdonald, took the news to a Mr Rutherford, who rode to nearby Wangaratta and raised the alarm. Morgan was shot from behind, through the throat, early the next morning; he did not die until about 2 p.m. The mutilation of the body after death did take place. A Dr Henry of Benalla shaved off Morgan's beard and said he would have a tobacco pouch made from the hair. Souvenir hunters cut so many locks of his hair off that he was practically bald. The head was

THE DEATH OF MORGAN
oil on hardboard 35 cm x 45 cm 1976

eventually shaved and then cut from the body, pickled in brine and sent to Professor George Halford of Melbourne University, who made a death mask for the university museum.

The Morning of the Fray

"Come on, boys!" says the Darkie, with the devil in his eye;
  "Come, blacken up, get ready: for ere the fall of night,
We've merry work before us—we've got to do or die;
  At Eugowra Rocks ere sundown, we've got to fall or fight.
We'll stop the Orange escort with powder and with ball,
  Lift the diggers' money and collar all the gold,
Smash the coach to pieces, and down the peelers all—
  So mind your guns are killers, my comrades brave and bold:
There's only four policemen, and ten of us all told!"

Bang! Bang! go off the rifles: the battle has begun;
  Ah! See the escort running; and now the robbers bold
Seize upon the plunder, and with the setting sun
  They're riding from Eugowra encumbered with the gold.
And as with savage laughter they leave the fated place,
  Gardiner—that's "the Darkie"—is shouting loud, "Hooray!"
"Hooray! We've struck bonanza; we've won the steeplechase—
  I think we've made our fortunes at Eugowra Rocks today."
And so with wicked jesting, the outlaws rode away.

ANON.

Note: Frank Gardiner, a half-caste Aboriginal, had a long and very exciting career. He was a ruthless man, and combined the qualities of bravery and leadership. After he went north to Queensland (where he was later arrested) he led a blameless life until he was captured. He was sentenced to a long term of imprisonment, but was later reprieved and exiled. He died in California. There is another poem here about him, telling of his arrest and sentence.

The Eugowra Rocks robbery was the first hold-up of a major gold escort in New South Wales. Tom Roberts painted a famous oil of the incident, very close to the site of the actual robbery.

This poem comes from Charles Macalister's book, Old Pioneering Days in the Sunny South, *in which Macalister says it was written by Gardiner, but most authorities do not agree that this was possible.*

THE MORNING OF THE FRAY
oil on hardboard 36 cm x 43 cm 1976

Frank Gardiner

Frank Gardiner, he is caught at last and now in Sydney jail—
For wounding Sergeant Middleton and robbing the Mudgee mail,
For plundering of the escort and the Carcoar mail also,
It was for gold he made so bold, and not so long ago.

His daring deeds surprised them all throughout our Sydney land;
He gave a call unto his friends and quickly raised a band.
Fortune always favoured him until the time of late;
There was Burke, the brave O'Meally too, met with a dreadful fate.

Young Johnny Vane surrendered, Ben Hall received some wounds;
And as for Johnny Gilbert, near Binalong he was found.
Alone he was, he lost his horse, three troopers hove in sight;
He fought the three most manfully, got slaughtered in the fight.

Farewell, adieu to outlawed Frank, he was the poor man's friend;
The Government has secured him, the laws he did offend.
He boldly stood his trial and answered in a breath,
"Do what you will, you can but kill. I have no fear of death!"

Fresh charges brought against him from neighbours near and far;
Day after day they remanded him, escorted from the bar.
And now it is all over, the sentence it is passed,
Reprieving from the gallows cursed this highwayman at last.

When lives you take—a warning boys—a woman never trust.
She will turn round, I will be bound, Queen's Evidence the first.
Two and thirty years he's doomed to slave all for the Crown;
And well may he say he cursed the day he met with Kitty Brown.

ANON.

Note: After the Eugowra robbery, Gardiner, accompanied by Mrs Kitty Brown, left New South Wales and settled as a storekeeper outside Rockhampton in Queensland on the road to the Canoona diggings. He was inadvertently given away by a letter written to her sister by Kitty Brown. The sister was, incidentally, married to Ben Hall, but living with an ex-policeman, who turned the letter over to the troopers for the reward offered for Gardiner. Gardiner served ten years of his sentence before being exiled to California, where he kept a saloon. He died in America. There is an apocryphal story that he was shot following a card game.

THE TRIAL OF GARDINER
oil on hardboard 36 cm x 49 cm 1976

The Diverting History of John Gilbert

John Gilbert was a bushranger
  Of terrible renown
For sticking lots of people up
  And shooting others down.

John Gilbert said unto his pals,
  "Although they make a bobbery
About our tricks, we've never done
  A tip-top thing in robbery.

"We've all of us a fancy for
  Experiments in pillage;
But never have we seized a town,
  Or even sacked a village."

John Gilbert stated to his mates,
  "Though partners we have been
In all rascality, yet we
  No festal day have seen."

John Gilbert said he thought he saw
  No obstacle to hinder a
Piratical descent upon
  The town of Canowindra.

So into Canowindra town
  Rode Gilbert and his men,
And all the Canowindra folk
  Subsided there and then.

The Canowindra populace
  Cried, "Here's a lot of strangers,"
But suddenly recovered when
  They found they were bushrangers.

John Gilbert with his partisans
  Said, "Don't you be afraid—
We are but old companions whom
  Rank outlaws you have made."

So Johnny Gilbert says, says he,
  "We'll never hurt a hair
Of men who bravely recognise
  That we are just and fair."

The New South Welshmen said at once,
  Not making any fuss,
That Johnny Gilbert, after all,
  Was "just but one of us".

THE DIVERTING HISTORY OF JOHN GILBERT I
oil on hardboard 36 cm x 49 cm 1976

So Johnny Gilbert took the town
  And all the public houses,
And treated all the cockatoos
  And shouted for their spouses.

And Miss O'Flanagan performed
  In manner quite "ginteely"
Upon the grand piano for
  The bushranger O'Meally.

And every stranger passing by
  They took, and when they'd got him,
They robbed him of his money, and
  Occasionally shot him.

And Johnny's enigmatic freak
  Admits of this solution,
Bushranging is in New South Wales
  A favoured institution.

So Johnny Gilbert ne'er allows
  An anxious thought to fetch him,
Because he knows the Government
  Don't really want to catch him.

And if such practices should be
  To New South Welshmen dear,
With not the least demurring word
  Ought we to interfere?

ANON.

Note: Ben Hall, John Gilbert (alias, Roberts, a Canadian immigrant), and John O'Meally, held up the town of Canowindra in N.S.W. for three days, from 17 to 20 October 1863. While Hall was the leader of the gang, the anonymous parodist obviously wanted to get as close as possible to the English poem "John Gilpin", which he parodied so neatly. From the tone of the verse, the author was almost certainly a Victorian!

THE DIVERTING HISTORY OF JOHN GILBERT II
oil on hardboard 35 cm x 45 cm 1976

The Death of Ben Hall

Ben Hall was out on the Lachlan side
  With a thousand pounds on his head;
A score of troopers were scattered wide
  And a hundred more were ready to ride
Wherever a rumour led.

They had followed his track from the Weddin
    heights
  And north by the Weelong yards;
Through dazzling days and moonlit nights
  They had sought him over their rifle sights
With their hands on the trigger-guards.

The outlaw stole like a hunted fox
  Through the scrub and stunted heath,
And peered like a hawk from his eyrie rocks
  Through the waving boughs of the sapling box
On the troopers riding beneath.

His clothes were rent by the clutching thorn
  And his blistered feet were bare;
Ragged and torn, with his beard unshorn,
  He hid in the woods like a beast forlorn
With a padded path to his lair.

But every night when the white stars rose
  He crossed by the Gunning Plain
To a stockman's hut where the Gunning flows,
  And struck on the door three swift light blows,
And a hand unhooked the chain—

And the outlaw followed the lone path back
  With food for another day;
And the kindly darkness covered his track
  And the shadows swallowed him deep and black
Where the starlight melted away.

But his friend had read of the Big Reward
  And his soul was stirred with greed;
He fastened his door and window-board,
  He saddled his horse and crossed the ford,
And spurred to the town at speed.

You may ride at a man or a maid's behest
  When honour or true love call
And steel your heart to the worst or best,
  But the ride that is ta'en on a traitor's quest
Is the bitterest ride of all.

THE DEATH OF BEN HALL I
oil on hardboard 35 cm x 45 cm 1976

A hot wind blew from the Lachlan bank
  And a curse on its shoulder came;
The pine-trees frowned at him, rank on rank,
  The sun on a gathering storm-cloud sank
And flushed his cheek with shame.

He reined at the Court, and the tale began
  That the rifles alone should end;
Sergeant and trooper laid their plan
  To draw the net on a hunted man
At the treacherous word of a friend.

False was the hand that raised the chain
  And false was the whispered word:
"The troopers have turned to the south again,
  You may dare to camp on the Gunning Plain."
And the weary outlaw heard.

He walked from the hut but a quarter-mile
  Where a clump of saplings stood
In a sea of grass like a lonely isle;
  And the moon came up in a little while
Like silver steeped in blood.

Ben Hall lay down on the dew-wet ground
  By the side of his tiny fire;
And a night-breeze woke, and he heard no sound
  As the troopers drew their cordon round—
And the traitor earned his hire.

And nothing they saw in the dim grey light
  But the little glow in the trees;
And they crouched in the tall cold grass all night,
  Each one ready to shoot on sight,
With his rifle cocked on his knees.

When the shadows broke, and the dawn's white sword
  Swung over the mountain wall,
And a little wind blew over the ford
  A Sergeant sprang to his feet and roared,
"In the name of the Queen, Ben Hall!"

Haggard, the outlaw leapt from his bed
  With his lean arms held on high.
"Fire!" And the words were scarcely said
  When the mountains rang to a rain of lead—
And the dawn went drifting by.

THE DEATH OF BEN HALL II
oil on hardboard 35 cm x 45 cm 1976

They kept their word and they paid his pay
  Where a clean man's hand would shrink;
And that was the traitor's master day
  As he stood by the bar on his homeward way
And called on the crowd to drink.

He banned no creed and he barred no class,
  And he called to his friends by name;
But the worst would shake his head and pass,
  And none would drink from the bloodstained
    glass
And the goblet red with shame.

And I know when I hear the last grim call
  And my mortal hour is spent,
When the light is hid and the curtains fall
  I would rather sleep with the dead Ben Hall
Than go where that traitor went.

ANON.

Note: This is a fairly accurate account of Hall's betrayal by Michael Connolly, at Forbes, on 5 May 1865. "Goobong Mick", as he was known, had acted as one of Hall's "telegraphs" and "bankers" for some years. It is possible that he had some of the proceeds of Hall's robberies banked in his name, and this, as well as the reward, might have tempted him to betray the outlaw. The anonymous versifier shows some skill in his work, and this is more likely to have been written by an English immigrant than many of the more rough ballads; see, for instance, the use of the word "woods" in line four, stanza four, where an Australian might have used "bush". The poem that follows describes the arrival of Hall's body in Forbes, and may have been written on the same day by John McGuire. There is a tradition to this effect. I have seen the man's name given as "Coobong", "Goobong" and "Goobang" Mick Connolly.

THE DEATH OF BEN HALL III
oil on hardboard 35 cm x 45 cm 1976

The Streets of Forbes

Come all you Lachlan men, a sorrowful tale I'll tell,
  Concerning a bold hero, who through misfortune fell.
His name it was Ben Hall, a man of high renown
  Who was hunted from his station and like a dog shot
    down.

Three years he roamed the highway and had a lot of fun,
  A thousand pounds was on his head, with Gilbert and
    John Dunn.

Ben parted from his comrades, and they did all agree
  To give up their bushranging and cross the stormy sea.

Ben went to Goobang Creek, and that was his downfall;
  For riddled like a sieve was valiant Ben Hall.
It was early in the morning upon the fifth of May
  The troopers gathered round him, as fast asleep he lay.

Bill Dargin he was chosen to shoot the outlaw dead;
  The troopers fired madly and filled him full of lead.
They threw him on his horse and strapped him like a swag,
  Then led him through the streets of Forbes, to show the
    prize they had.

JOHN McGUIRE(?)

See the notes for the preceding ballad.

THE STREETS OF FORBES
oil on hardboard 35 cm x 45 cm 1976

The Maryborough Miner

Come all you sons of liberty and listen to my song.
I'll tell you my occupations and it won't take very long.
I've travelled around this countryside, ten thousand miles or more;
And many's the time I might have starved, but for the cheek I bore.

I came to the Fitzroy River, boys, all with my Bendigo rig;
I had a shovel, a pick and a dish, and for a licence I begged
But the Assayman called me a loafer, said for work I'd no desire,
And so to do him justice, boys, I set his office on fire.

Oh, yes, my jolly jokers, I've done it on the cross.
Although I hump my bluey today, I've sweated many a horse.
I've helped to rob the escort of many an ounce of gold,
And the traps have trailed upon my tail more times than I ever told.

Oh, yes, the traps have trailed me and been frightened out of their stripes.
They never tried to catch me for they feared my cure for gripes.
And well they knew I carried it, for they had often seen
It glistening in my flipper, chaps, my patent "pill-machine".

I'm one of the men that starved upon a reef at Tarangower,
Anxiety and misery my grim companions there.
I've puddled the clay at Bendigo, and chanced my arm at Kew,
And wound up my avocations with ten years on Cockatoo.

And now I must be going, it's time to move along,
Just an old lag remembering the times that are long gone;
And you must understand, my lads, just from my little rhyme
I'm a Maryborough miner, and one of the good old time.

ANON.

Note: I first heard a version of this song sung by A. L. Lloyd on a Wattle recording. He did not give a source for it. It has much in common with a set of verses in Paterson's Old Bush Songs *called "The Murrumbidgee Shearer", which could certainly be sung to the same tune. I have inserted the first two lines of the last verse, adapting them from another old song, "The Old Keg Of Rum"; this was to round out an incomplete verse.*

THE MARYBOROUGH MINER
oil on hardboard 35 cm x 45 cm 1976

Thunderbolt

Thunderbolt came from the Hawkesbury River,
He was a bushranger, he was a rover;
Made all the rich folk shudder and shiver,
Wore fine clothes and lived in clover.
Riding high on a thoroughbred colt,
Bad man, bushranger,
Thunderbolt.

Uralla, Armidale, Torrington as well,
Yarrowick Mountain where the farmers dwell,
Saw him pass; till a constable in blue,
Caught him and sent him to Cockatoo.
But he broke from his cell
And his iron chain,
And he wandered free
In the bush again.

He wandered far, he wandered wide,
Nobody knows just where he died,
But on Yarrowick Mountain when the moon is high
And misty clouds are drifting by,
Riding high
On his thoroughbred colt,
Comes the ghost of Thunderbolt.
Comes the ghost of Thunderbolt. . .

W. N. SCOTT

Note: As with some other bushrangers, there are stories that the man killed by Constable Walker was not Fred Ward at all. A woman called Annie Rixon wrote a whole book about this, called Captain Thunderbolt. *I have never been able to trace who she was, or her motive for writing the book, though I possess a copy. This was written as a poem for my own children, and is effective if the last verse is read softly when you read the poem aloud.*

THUNDERBOLT
oil on hardboard 35 cm x 45 cm 1976

A Day's Ride

Bold are the mounted robbers who on stolen horses ride
And bold the mounted troopers who patrol the Sydney side;
But few of them, though flash they be, can ride, and few can fight
As Walker did, for life and death, with Ward the other night.

It seems the troopers heard that Ward, well known as Thunderbolt,
An outlawed thief, was down near Blanche to try a fresh-roped colt.
(Not far from Armidale, that spot for brilliants so renowned—
Although the talked-of diamonds seldom now are found.)

Said Alec Walker as he clapped his saddle on his steed,
"If I catch sight of Ward today, I'll try his horse's speed;
Uphill or down, 'tis all the same, I know my nag can stay"—
Then got his arms and galloped off, all ready for the fray.

Soon as he got near Thunderbolt, the first salute he got
From that retreating party was a random pistol-shot;
The robber fled, the trooper went in chase, his spirits rose—
When Ward advised him to keep off, he answered, "Bosh, here
  goes!"

As through the scrubby bush they sped, and timbertangled brake,
Both held their horses well in hand, nor made the least mistake;
Easing his horse with judgement then, the light-weight trooper
  raced—
Good jockey as the robber was, he found himself outpaced.

Mile after mile, rough ground and smooth, up hill and down the vale,
Steep rocky tracks they galloped o'er—Ward's horse began to fail.
Scant time he had for firing, for whenever he looked back
Onward his adversary pressed, fast nearing on his track.

On to a creek pursuer and pursued still headed straight:
One hastening to avenge the law, his foe to meet his fate.
Ward, almost hopeless of escape, devised a desperate scheme—
Dismounting from his horse he swam the wide and rapid stream.

Cried Walker, "May my mother's son forever be accursed
If now I fail to take him, but I'll stop his gallop first."
His pistol flashed, the stockhorse fell; cut off from all retreat
At bay the reckless outlaw stood, defiant in defeat.

"I'll not surrender," was his cry; "before I do, I'll die!"
"All right," his brave opponent said, "now for it, you or I!"
A moment's pause—a parley now—the trooper made a push
To grapple at close quarters with the ranger of the bush.

A DAY'S RIDE
oil on hardboard 35 cm x 45 cm 1976

A shot—a blow—a struggle wild—the outlaw with a shriek
Relaxed his hold and sank below the waters of the creek.
'Twas thus the dreaded robber's evil spirit passed away,
Vanquished by brave young Walker, the hero of the day.

Henceforth those loafing swagmen who around the stations coil,
Exchanging lies at night until they see the billies boil,
At lambing-down or shearing-time, will tell with bated breath
Of Walker's fight with Thunderbolt, that fight for life and death.

ANON.

Note: This encounter took place about 26 May 1870. Walker was accompanied by another trooper, named Mulhall, whose horse bolted with him at the first exchange of shots. He got it under control and chased Ward's companion, whom he captured alive. Walker encountered Ward near a deep waterhole in a creek bed, and shot his horse. Ward took to the water like an old man kangaroo, and warned Walker off. They exchanged shots, and Ward was wounded. Walker dismounted, and dragged him from the water, and believing him to be dead, laid the body out on the grass and went for assistance to Blanche's Hotel, to get a cart to bring the body in. On reaching the river they found the bushranger had disappeared. It being by this time too dark to follow tracks, they waited for dawn, and followed the blood spoor to a clump of bushes where Thunderbolt lay dead. During his seven years of outlawry, Thunderbolt never killed a man. On one occasion he held up a German band and not only robbed them but made them perform for him. They pleaded for their little money, and he said that if he successfully stole a racehorse he was after he would post their money back to them. He later sent them a postal order for twenty pounds to Warwick in Queensland.

The Death of Peter Clark

The sun was blazing fiercely on the cracked and dusty plain
As Peter Clark the drover rode toward his home again.
For weeks he'd been a-droving where the golden sunsets glow,
Behind the lowing cattle of a trail-herd moving slow.
With stockwhip ringing loudly as the breaking steer he wheeled
And curses shouted fiercely at the yapping dogs that heeled,
He'd taken cattle safely from his Lower Hunter home,
To where the Namoi River waters fields of reddened loam.

He rode with one companion, a lad of fifteen years;
A gamer little stockman never cracked a whip at steers;
For when the herd was fractious or it broke in wild stampede
He'd ride to wheel the leaders and the danger never heed.
The lad could sit an outlaw till "the sky was underneath",
Whose eyes would roll and whiten as it bared the wicked teeth.
While saddle-girths were creaking with the sudden reefs and strains,
He'd sink the spur-rowels deeply as he loosed the foam-flecked
reins.

The drovers rode in silence to the distant range of blue,
Where rise the giant Murrulla and the towering Tinagroo
In solitary grandeur, mighty monarchs of the range
That reign, their might unchallenged, o'er a kingdom wild and
strange.
Like sentinels that guard the plains their rugged summits rise
Against the dim horizon, as in challenge to the skies;
And o'er the mighty gorges with a misty mantle hung
The soaring eagle circles o'er her unmolested young.

As on the drovers travelled through the lazy afternoon
The youngster's heart was happy and he gaily hummed a tune;
But Clark was grim and silent, as the horse he loved to ride
Moved on toward the ranges with a long and springy stride.
For early in the morning when they paused their mounts to change,
A squad of mounted troopers coming back from Warland's Range
Had said that dreaded Wilson, just a day or two before,
Had swooped and robbed the mail coach of the golden freight it
bore.

They warned the elder drover, but his laugh was cold and strange,
For well he knew, that evening, they must camp on Warland's
Range.
As, winding up, the roadway passed where range and foothill met,
The drover knew they'd reach the spot just as the sun was set;
But loudly had he boasted that they'd camp on yonder hill:
No man in all the country could his heart with terror fill.
He'd camp, in spite of Wilson, when the evening sun was low
And o'er the gloomy ranges cast its last departing glow.

The troopers had not argued, for they knew the drover well,
And knew he'd never waver at a devil straight from hell—
As tough and game a fighter as the country ever knew,
He'd fought on every stockroute from the coast to the Barcoo,
And never man could stop him when across the overland
He rode behind the cattle with that burnt and hardy band,
When drovers had to battle for the starving stock to pass
And squatters fought to keep them from the brown and dying grass.

They reached the camp as darkness cast her shadows o'er the ground
And soon the weary horses grazed contented close around.
The drovers by the fireside sat and drank their billy tea,
While round about the hobble chains were clinking cheerily.
They talked of home and people, as the gentle evening breeze
Would waft the smoke in spirals through the branches of the trees,
Till, tired, they sought the solace of the peaceful land of sleep,
And never dreamed that danger through the silent night would
creep.

But through the inky darkness came a sharp and stern command;
The drovers from their blankets were compelled to rise and stand—
Each man to face the shadow with his hands above his head;
One move, the man informed them, and he'd riddle them with lead.
But Clark was calm and silent, as the outlaw came in sight;
His thoughts were fast revolving, for he meant to rush and fight;
And as the dreaded Wilson sought the plucky drover's gold,
He sprang with arms extended seeking for a fatal hold.

A gunshot stabbed the darkness with a crimson jet of flame,
The wounded drover staggered, but he came on just the same,
And closed upon the outlaw with a grip of tempered steel;
His blood was flowing freely but the wound he did not feel.
He strained and wrestled fiercely as he fought to gain a holt
Upon the arm of Wilson and the hand that held the "Colt".
But in the deadly struggle, fate must play a leading part—
The gun, again exploding, shot the drover through the heart.

The drover fell, but falling, threw his powerful arms around
The body of the outlaw as they crashed upon the ground;
And thus the plucky drover drew a last and fleeting breath,
With Wilson locked unconscious in the mighty grip of death.
The youngster, dumb with terror, as the two had fought and
strained,
Had watched the battle, helpless, but his mind he now regained;
And rushing to his saddle for a length of greenhide rope
He bound the two together where they lay upon the slope.

Then, mounting quickly, galloped through the darkness of the night
To tell the mounted troopers of the drover's fatal fight.
With hoofbeats ringing loudly as the spur at every stride
Left blood from flank to shoulder on the sweating horse's side,

THE DEATH OF PETER CLARK I
oil on hardboard 35 cm x 45 cm 1976

He brought the racing troopers, till the light of breaking day
Revealed the bloody camp-site, where in death the drover lay,
Wrapped sound in sleep eternal with his days of droving o'er,
Still tightly locked with Wilson, who would scourge the range no
more.

And o'er the saddened country spread the tidings far and wide;
The mountain breezes mourning through the wattle blossom sighed;
But on the Lower Hunter, where the swaying willows sweep,
A someone's heart was bleeding for a drover wrapped in sleep.
Through Wingen, Scone and Blanford spread the story of the death,
And far away to westward, where the summer's scorching breath
The dying herbage withers, where the rolling plains are wide,
And horses groan and labour, as the teamster rides beside.

HUBERT H. PARRY ("BARWON")

Note: This is founded in fact, though the true story is very different from that told in the poem. In April 1864, three brothers named Peter, James and Acton Clarke accompanied by a boy of twelve years were held up near Culgoa, near Warland's Range, by a bushranger named Harry Wilson, aged twenty. Peter Clarke did attack the man, and was fatally shot in the struggle; James Clarke and the boy, whose name was Conroy, were both wounded also. The bushranger was overcome and taken to Maitland, where he was convicted and hung for wilful murder, in October 1864. A monument was raised by public subscription to the memory of Peter Clarke's brave act, and it stands at Murrurundi.

THE DEATH OF PETER CLARK II
oil on hardboard 35 cm x 45 cm 1976

A Night's Walk

Power, the noted highwayman, had long disturbed the peace
Throughout this country, not to speak of baffling the police;
Though numbers strove to capture him, yet all contrived to fail
And none this bird could catch to sprinkle salt upon his tail.

Long time the Captain of Police reflected in despair,
At last he thought of Nicholson, De Montfort, and of Hare;
All men inured to peril, sons of a warlike race,
Men never known to shrink from looking danger in the face.

Forth rode these heroes of the Force that Longmore glorified,
Intent on steadfast duty, and with them went a guide,
Three days in preparation spent, they first contrived their plan,
And then their search for Power in reality began.

For three more weary days they rode, and none but must applaud
The way the mountain ranges and rough country was explored
With patient perseverance; while they studied all the time
To guard against "bush telegraphs" who sympathize with crime.

Full many a mountain stream they crossed, swollen o'er by months of rain—
Such roads they never tracked before, and ne'er may see again;
Through rain, through dark, through pathless bush, still onwardly they toiled,
Half starved and wet, they only feared their object might be foiled.

All day, all night, they travelled on, and closely searched the ground
To see if any traces of the outlaw might be found.
At length they left their horses and pushed on through thick and thin
Until they reached the station of the cattle-fancier Quinn.

With outmost caution, one by one, they past the station crept,
Favoured by rain and darkness while the very watchdogs slept;
All night they searched; at break of day the guide in whispers spoke
When almost hopeless of success, "We've got him, there's a smoke!"

A moment's reconnoitre, on rushed the valiant Three,
And seized the well armed robber, who could neither fight nor flee,
But, taken by complete surprise, screamed wildly in despair,
Finding himself a prisoner in this his safest lair.

He told his captors had he known, their visit he'd have stopped,
And long before they reached his camp, some of them he'd have dropped,
Then said he wished to die quite game and begged he might be shot
(It being the open season now), but they thought better not.

A NIGHT'S WALK
oil on hardboard 35 cm x 45 cm 1976

They next sat down to breakfast, of which they stood in need
Through having gone some thirty hours, or more, without a feed;
Then took their man to Beechworth jail, and ended the career
Of Power who'd roamed the bush at large for very near a year.

Against the Force let Longmore still his angry passions vent,
And underrate the hardships these heroes underwent,
Which, borne without a murmur, so many nights and days,
With utmost pluck and patience too, demand our highest praise.

ANON.

Note: Henry Johnson, alias "Old Harry" Power, escaped from Pentridge where he was serving fourteen years for horse stealing in February 1869, and was active on the roads for 16 months. There is an apocryphal story that he took the young Ned Kelly along to act as horseholder while he held up coaches. At least the Beechworth police charged the young Kelly with this, but the charges were dismissed for lack of evidence. Power had his hideout on "Glenmore", a station owned by Ned Kelly's grandfather, James Quinn, near the King River in Victoria. He was sold out to the police for the reward of five hundred pounds offered for Power's capture. Power relied on the informant Jack Lloyd, who had been a fellow prisoner in Pentridge with him and was married to Ned Kelly's aunt, his mother's sister. But mostly he relied on a peacock that was kept at the Quinn homestead and was better than a watchdog, screaming loudly so as to be heard for miles if a stranger approached. Jack Lloyd, accompanied by Superintendents Hare and Nicholson, Sergeant Montford and a black tracker, stole past the Quinn homestead in heavy rain at night without waking the peacock, and took Power in his humpy of bark slabs. The old man offered no resistance, even offering his captors a cup of tea. He was convicted and sentenced to fifteen years, which he served. Later he became caretaker (in 1885) of a hulk called the Success *which was moored in Port Phillip as a floating museum. He was accidentally drowned while holidaying at Swan Hill in November 1891. Jack Lloyd died long before; he either fell or was pushed from his horse in the Kelly country, where informers could not expect a long life, or a peaceful one. Power firmly believed that Ned Kelly was the informer, and gave him away to be released from the charges brought against him, but the police admitted that the informer was Lloyd after his death.*

Stringybark Creek

A Sergeant and three constables set out from Mansfield town
Near the end of last October for to hunt the Kellys down;
They started for the Wombat Hills and thought it quite a lark
When they camped upon the borders of a creek called Stringybark.

They had grub and ammunition there to last them many a week
And next morning two of them rode out, all to explore the creek,
Leaving McIntyre behind them at the camp to cook the grub
And Lonergan to sweep the floor and boss the washingtub.

It was shortly after breakfast Mac thought he heard a noise
So gun in hand he sallied out to try and find the cause,
But he never saw the Kellys planted safe behind a log
So he sauntered back to smoke and yarn and wire into the prog.

But Ned Kelly and his comrades thought they'd like a nearer look,
For being short of grub they wished to interview the cook;
And of firearms and cartridges they found they had too few,
So they longed to grab the pistols and ammunition too.

Both the troopers at a stump alone they were well pleased to see
Watching as the billies boiled to make their pints of tea;
There they joked and chattered gaily never thinking of alarms
Till they heard the fearful cry behind, "Bail up! Throw up your
arms!"

The traps they started wildly, and Mac then firmly stood
While Lonergan made tracks to try and gain the wood,
Reaching round for his revolver, but before he touched the stock
Ned Kelly pulled the trigger, fired, and dropped him like a rock.

Then after searching McIntyre all through the camp they went
And cleared the guns and cartridges and pistols from the tent,
But brave Kelly muttered sadly as he loaded up his gun,
"Oh, what a bloody pity that the bastard tried to run!"

'Twas later in the afternoon the Sergeant and his mate
Came riding blithely through the bush to meet a cruel fate.
"The Kellys have the drop on you!" cried McIntyre aloud,
But the troopers took it as a joke and sat their horses proud.

Then Trooper Scanlan made a move his rifle to unsling,
But to his heart a bullet sped and death was in the sting;
Then Kennedy leapt from his mount and ran for cover near,
And fought, a game man to the last, for all that life held dear.

The Sergeant's horse raced from the camp, alike from friend and
foe,
And McIntyre, his life at stake, sprang to the saddlebow

And galloped far into the night, a haunted, harassed soul,
Then like a hunted bandicoot, hid in a wombat hole.

At dawn of day he hastened forth and made for Mansfield town
To break the news that made men vow to shoot the bandits down,
So from that hour the Kelly gang was hunted far and wide,
Like outlawed dingoes of the wild until the day they died.

ANON.

Note: Until the brutal murders described above, the Kellys were looked upon as offenders, and stock thieves, but there was not a great deal of bitterness toward them among the Mounted Police. The same could not be said about the Foot Police, some of whom hated the Kellys and other settlers of their kind as horse and cattle thieves and troublemakers. But the Stringybark Creek episode led to the Kellys' being officially outlawed, and a reward of two thousand pounds being offered for their apprehension. Incidentally, Ned Kelly was so impressed by the bravery of Sergeant Kennedy that he walked a quarter of a mile back to the camp to get a cloak to cover the body. The other bodies were left uncovered. Kelly afterwards told Aaron Sherritt that Kennedy was the bravest man he had ever met.

STRINGYBARK CREEK
oil on hardboard 35 cm x 45 cm 1976

The Kelly Gang

Oh, Paddy dear, and did you hear the news that's going round,
On the head of bold Ned Kelly they have placed two thousand pound.
And on Steve Hart, Joe Byrne and Dan, two thousand more they'd give,
But if the price was doubled, boys, the Kelly gang would live.

'Tis hard to think such plucky hearts in crime should be employed.
'Tis by police prosecution they have all been much annoyed.
Revenge is sweet, and in the bush they can defy the Law;
Such sticking up and plundering you never saw before.

'Twas in November, Seventy-eight, when the Kelly gang came down,
Just after shooting Kennedy, to famed Euroa town.
To rob the bank of all its gold was their idea that day;
Blood-horses they were mounted on to make their getaway.

So Kelly marched into the bank, a cheque all in his hand,
For to have it changed for money of Scott he did demand;
And when that he refused him, he, looking at him straight,
Said, "See here, my name's Ned Kelly, and this here man's my mate."

With pistols pointed at his nut poor Scott did stand amazed;
His stick he would have liked to cut, but was with fear half crazed.
The poor cashier, with real fear stood trembling at the knees,
But at last they both seen 'twas no use, and handed out the keys.

The safe was quickly gutted then, the drawers turned out as well,
The Kellys being quite polite like any noble swell.
With flimsies, gold and silver coin, the threepennies and all
Amounting to two thousand pounds they made a glorious haul.

"Now hand out all your firearms," the robber boldly said,
"And all your ammunition or a bullet through your head.
Now, get your wife and children—come man, now look alive;
All jump into this buggy and we'll take you for a drive."

They took them to a station about three miles away,
And kept them close imprisoned until the following day.
The owner of the station and those in his employ
And a few unwary travellers their company did enjoy.

An Indian hawker fell in too, as everybody knows;
He came in handy to the gang by fitting them with clothes.
Then with their worn-out clothing they made a few bonfires,
And then destroyed the telegraph by cutting down the wires.

THE KELLY GANG I
oil on hardboard 35 cm x 45 cm 1976

Oh, Paddy dear, do shed a tear, I can't but sympathize;
Those Kellys are the devils, for they've made another rise;
This time across the billabong on Morgan's ancient beat,
They've robbed the banks of thousands, and in safety did retreat.

The matter may be serious, Pat, but still I can't but laugh,
To think the tales the bobbies told must all amount to chaff.
They said they had them all hemmed in, they could not get away,
But they turned up in New South Wales, and made the journey pay!

They rode into Jerilderie town at twelve o'clock at night,
Aroused the troopers from their beds and gave them an awful fright.
They took them in their night-shirts, ashamed I am to tell,
They covered them with revolvers and locked them in a cell.

They next acquainted the women-folk that they were going to stay,
And take possession of the camp until the following day.
They fed their horses in the stalls without the slightest fear,
Then went to rest their weary limbs till daylight did appear.

Next morning being Sunday morn, of course they must be good;
They dressed themselves in troopers' clothes, and Ned, he chopped
 some wood.
No one there suspected them, as troopers they did pass,
And Dan, the most religious one, took the sergeant's wife to Mass.

They spent the day most pleasantly, had plenty of good cheer,
Fried beef-steak and onions, tomato sauce and beer;
The ladies in attendance indulged in pleasant talk,
And just to ease the troopers' minds, they took them for a walk.

On Monday morning early, still masters of the ground,
They took their horses to the forge and had them shod all round;
Then back they came and mounted, their plans all laid so well,
In company with the troopers they stuck up the Royal Hotel.

They bailed up all the occupants and placed them in a room,
Saying, "Do as we command you or death will be your doom."
A Chinese cook "No savvy!" cried, not knowing what to fear,
But they brought him to his senses with a lift under the ear.

All who now approached the house just shared a similar fate,
In hardly any time at all the number was twenty-eight.
They shouted freely for all hands, and paid for all they drank,
And two of them remained in charge, and two went to the bank.

The farce was here repeated as I've already told,
They bailed up all the banker's clerks and robbed them of their gold.
The manager could not be found, and Kelly, in great wrath,
Searched high and low, and luckily he found him in his bath.

THE KELLY GANG II
oil on hardboard 35 cm x 45 cm 1976

The robbing o'er, they mounted then, to make a quick retreat,
They swept away with all their loot by Morgan's ancient beat;
And where they've gone, I do not know, if I did I wouldn't tell,
So now, until I hear from them, I'll bid you all farewell!

ANON.

Note: This is a very close description of the raids on Euroa and Jerilderie by the Kellys, and follows closely the actual incidents. It must have been written soon after the events described, and by someone who knew a lot, for even the food described as being eaten at the police station at Jerilderie is listed. The "station, about three miles away" from Euroa, was Younghusband's station, and the Kellys had taken it on Monday 18 December 1878, to use as a base for their robbery of the bank. The hawker was not "an Indian hawker" but a white man called Gloster, and he turned up on the Monday. The gang outfitted themselves from the stock in his cart, and took all the firearms he had. The station workers and Gloster were locked up and held in a strong storehouse, fed regularly and let out for a breath of air at intervals. The women were not molested or abused in any way. On Tuesday afternoon the party in the storehouse had been increased by eight, four gentlemen who had been driving, and four navvies from the railway gang who objected to the gang tearing down the telegraph wires. The bank was robbed just on closing time on Tuesday. The manager, Mr Scott, was held at pistol point while the bank was robbed. Then the clerk, Scott, his wife and family and the domestic servants were loaded into two carts, and the procession left for Younghusband's station. On the way they passed a large party of the townsfolk returning from a funeral at the local cemetery, but such was the ascendancy gained by the gang that no alarm was given. The prisoners were added to those in the store when they arrived at the station, and the gang left at about half-past eight at night, after warning the prisoners not to move for three hours. Once again, Kelly seems to have had such moral suasion that no move was made until half-past ten. The account of the Jerilderie affair also closely follows actual happenings.

THE KELLY GANG III
oil on hardboard 35 cm x 45 cm 1976

The Ballad of Jack Lefroy

Come all you lads and listen, a story I would tell,
Before they take me out and hang me high,
My name is Jack Lefroy, and life I would enjoy,
But the old judge has sentenced me to die.
My mother she was Irish and she taught me at her knee,
But to steady work I never did incline,
As a youngster I could ride, any horse was wrapped in hide,
And when I saw a good one, he was mine.

"Go straight, young man," they told me when my first long stretch was done,
"If you're jugged again, you'll have yourself to thank!"
But I swore I'd not be found hunting nuggets in the ground
When the biggest could be picked up in the bank.
Well, I've stuck up some mail-coaches, and I've ridden with Ben Hall,
And they never got me cornered once until
A pimp was in their pay gave my dingo-hole away
And they run me down to earth at Riley's Hill.

"Come out, Lefroy!" they called me. "Come out, we're five to one!"
But I took my pistols out and stood my ground.
For an hour I pumped out lead till they got me in the head,
And when I awoke they had me bound.
It's a pleasant way to live, boys, a gloomy way to die,
A-dangling with your neck inside a string—
How I'd like to ride again down the hills to Lachlan Plain!
But when the sun arises I must swing.

Chorus
So all young lads, take warning, and don't be led astray,
For the past you never, never can recall;
While young, your gifts employ, take a lesson from Lefroy,
Let his fate be a warning to you all.

ANON.

Note: I have never been able to trace the hanging of any bushranger called Lefroy, though it is possible that this could have been an alias used by one of Hall's followers, and the ballad written by someone who knew him by that name. Of the three main members of the Hall gang (Hall, Gilbert and Dunn), both Hall and Gilbert were shot to death by the police, and only Dunn was captured alive, though wounded (in the foot, not the head) and hung. He was just nineteen years of age. This could be an account, badly garbled, of the attack by police on Gilbert and Dunn at the Kelly homestead, though some of the facts do not fit the case.

The song is still extant. Stan Arthur collected a version of it near Brisbane in the late 1950s.

THE BALLAD OF JACK LEFROY
oil on hardboard 35 cm x 45 cm 1976

Bogong Jack and the Trooper

There's a story told about Bogong Jack
  And I won't go bail it's true,
But I ran across it a good while back
  And I'll pass it along to you.
He wasn't in Kelly's class, of course,
  Nor a hero like bold Ben Hall,
But he couldn't resist a beautiful horse,
  Branded or not, that's all.

This kept the traps in a state of strain
  From Omeo clear to Bright,
Till the squatters murmured they'd not complain
  If Bogong were shot on sight.
A constable on his promotion once
  Attempted to do just that
When he sighted his man by merest chance
  A mile above Clover Flat.

At the range it was probably hopeless, still
  It made his intention clear;
So Bogong bolted away uphill
  With the trap not far in the rear.
He went for the Kiewa Fork like smoke
  Where the creeks ran high with the rains,
For he reckoned the trap was a willing bloke
  But his mount might show more brains.

Smash through the water went Bogong Jack
  And patted his mare's wet skin,
But the trooper's horse at the brink shied back
  And the trooper went right in.
You shouldn't go into these mountain creeks
  Unless you're a mountain trout
For it may be a matter of days or weeks
  Before anyone hauls you out.

Well, the trooper wasn't. He simply clung
  To a rock with either hand,
And whenever the water bared his tongue
  He called upon Jack to "Stand!"
"Stand," said Jack, "I'd be grateful to,
  For it's been an exhausting game:
But it's hardly the thing for me to do
  When you can't do the same!"

"Are you going to be long in there? If so,
  I'll just have a bite and sup
From the saddlebag here. I should like to know
  How long you can keep it up!"

BOGONG JACK I
oil on hardboard 35 cm x 45 cm 1976

The trap gave in. He'd begun to feel
  Like one of the angler's worms,
So he kicked the boot from each waterlogged heel
  And accepted Bogong's terms.

He let his belt and his pouches drift,
  And settled himself to swim
On the blown-up water-bag, thoughtful gift
  Which Bogong handed him.
Bogong rode for a mile or more
  On the bank as he floated down,
Poling him carefully off the shore
  And seeing he didn't drown.

The trooper got home all right, it's said,
  But resigned from the Force next day
And his boots are down on the Kiewa's bed
  And there I suppose they'll stay.
This story may be a lot of tripe,
  But, if that's so, it's odd
That I once found a rowell of Government type
  In the craw of a Murray cod!

JOHN MANIFOLD

Note: Bogong Jack was probably an English migrant called John Payne. He was no hold-up man, and never murdered anybody, but he was a most accomplished horse and cattle-thief who is reputed to have been the first white man to discover a stock track through the Bogongs in Victoria. He stole stock on one side of the range, travelled them through to the other side, had them sold and was away before the word could come round! A book was written about his exploits by Eric Harding of Melbourne. John Manifold tells me he first heard this yarn about Bogong from an old bushman in his youth, and that he wrote it pretty much as he heard it, though I suspect the last four lines are of his own invention!

BOGONG JACK II
oil on hardboard 35 cm x 45 cm 1976

Bold Archibold Malone

There was a wild colonial boy, Jack Duggan was his name;
  They wrote a song about him, that's how he got his fame,
But we would like to tell you now of someone quite unknown—
  A terror to Australia called Archibald Malone.
Ranging through the bush and living off the land,
  His swag on his shoulder and his billy in his hand,
He was four foot eleven, of solid skin and bone;
  A microscopic outlaw was Archibald Malone.

Archibald Malone was a thieving son-of-a-gun,
  A wanted desperado, he was always on the run.
He'd been upon the run since his partner, Jock Magee,
  Put senna pods in his damper, and liquorice in his tea.
Ranging through the bush and living off the land,
  His swag on his shoulder and his billy in his hand;
He never wore his woolly vest when he was far from home—
  A worry to his mother was Archibald Malone.

He'd go and rob a bank when he had nothing else to do,
  He'd hold up a stage-coach to get a bob or two.
His daring feats of robbery were always in the news,
  He even picked the pockets of the local kangaroos.
Ranging through the bush and living off the land,
  His swag on his shoulder and his billy in his hand,
He never used deodorant, so he travelled all alone,
  That strong and pungent outlaw called Archibald Malone.

One day when he was cooking up some damper, cheese and pickle
  Up rode a trooper on a shiny motor-cicle.
"Come along with me, you haven't paid that parking fine,
  Your execution's Thursday and you'd better be on time!"
Ranging through the bush and living off the land,
  His swag on his shoulder and his billy in his hand.
"If you think you can do it, you can take me on your own,
  But I won't give up without a fight!" said Archibald Malone.

He grabbed his trusty pea-shooter and filled his mouth with peas,
  He fired them at the trooper, who hid behind the trees.
He grabbed another handful, fired another shot or two,
  But in his wild excitement, he sucked instead of blew!
And that was how young Archibald came to meet his death.
  He choked on the peas and he couldn't get his breath.
He choked until his face was purple and maroon;
  And that was how they captured him, brave Archibald Malone.

Ranging through the bush and living off the land,
  His swag on his shoulder, and his billy in his hand.
He strangled till his face was purple and maroon,
That technicolour outlaw, poor Archibald Malone.

DAVE WORTHINGTON